Forgive Yourself

Step Into Your Power

Illuminate Your Purpose

Replace Regret with Gratitude

Brenda Reiss

Limits of Liability and Disclaimer of Warranty

The author/publisher shall not be liable for your misuse of this material. This book is strictly for informational and educational purposes.

Warning – Disclaimer

The purpose of this book is to educate and entertain. It is distributed with the understanding that the publisher is not engaged in the dispensation of legal, psychological or any other professional advice. The content of each entry is the expression and opinion of its author and does not necessarily reflect the beliefs, practices or viewpoints of the publisher, its parent company or its affiliates. The publisher's choice to include any material within is not intended to express or imply any warranties or guarantees of any kind. The author and/or publisher do not guarantee that anyone following these techniques, suggestions, tips, ideas, or strategies will become successful. The author and/or publisher shall have neither liability nor responsibility to anyone with respect to any loss or damage caused, or alleged to be caused, directly or indirectly by the information contained in this book.

ISBN: 978-0-9740019-8-2

Get More of Brenda!

Download the free eBook
"11 Steps to Forgiveness"

Discover the key steps to bring about more joy in life.

In this book you will find how to:

- Bring more joy and peace to life.

- Practice healing through forgiveness.

- Use proven tools and techniques for getting started today!

Get the free eBook at **www.BrendaReissCoaching.com**

What Is Self-Forgiveness?

Self-forgiveness illuminates your true purpose—opening doors to healing your past while replacing regret with gratitude. Self-forgiveness enables more feelings of freedom, joy and inner peace.

What Is a Self-Forgiveness Coach?

As a Self-Forgiveness Coach, I help you create a path to endless possibilities by connecting the dots so you can re-write your story, stepping more fully into your own amazing power!

Find out more about how I can help you free yourself and find your true purpose at www.BrendaReissCoaching.com.

Brenda

Brenda Reiss

In Their Own Words

Hopeful for the First Time in a Very Long Time

"When I was introduced to Brenda and the Radical Forgiveness process I felt hopeful for the first time in a very long time! My life was spinning out of control and I had no answers, no direction, no hope. With Brenda's knowledge, insights and personal examples she takes all the uncertainty out and replaces it with a clear understanding of how it works for everyone! I would highly recommend working with Brenda for anyone who is also struggling with their life."

~Marilynn A.
Everett, WA

Honored to Be on This Journey with Brenda

"Brenda is patient and very generous with her time. She instinctually recognizes when I need time between lessons. I am still hard on myself, but she is always accepting of what is and lovingly encourages me to do the same. We laugh about one step forward and two backward. There are times that we are both amazed at my progress, yet she is careful not to take me further than I am ready to go. I find her instincts to be respectful and accurate. I'm honored to be on this journey with Brenda. With Brenda and her community, I am learning to receive the love."

~Joanne A.
Seattle, WA

Such an Amazing Process

"As a coach/teacher, Brenda is filled with so much caring and information, and had our groups and individual sessions thoroughly planned out. This was such an amazing process for me—not only being able to diffuse the misinformation and twisted truth that I had carried around, believing it to be my story, but to reframe the story and then be able to move on with a clearer and much lighter story. After years of much work in many areas this form of spiritual clearing and unblocking is so much better for me and helps me grow in so many areas."

~Michelle M.
Kirkland, WA

Happy, Joyful Life

"My husband and I were lucky enough to attend Brenda's group class. Brenda's blend of humor and compassion set the stage for open and honest conversations. We left each class with rich tools and guidance that, to this day, help us communicate, forgive, and move forward with a healthy and strong sense of self. When it comes down to it, it is the person in the mirror that needs our forgiveness to live a happy, joyful life. I highly recommend Brenda's council, workshops and book studies to anyone that wants to understand themselves and how self-image impacts relationships."

~Kathy S.
Renton, WA

Honored and Blessed

"I feel honored and blessed to have been part of Brenda's class. Brenda is a natural when it comes to being a great speaker! She is organized, loving, intuitive and pays attention to detail as well as to how people are feeling. The group connected so well and we all benefited from each other's insights and experiences. This study is a life changer and for the better. I highly recommend it. With Brenda's extensive background of training and personal skills, she is by far a teacher of excellence! Thank you, Brenda, so much!"

~Saacha B.
Snohomish, WA

Considerable Enlightenment and Relief

"I attended Brenda's class because I realized that I had a major self-forgiveness issue and was looking forward to resolving that issue. Throughout the book study, I experienced considerable enlightenment and relief. Now I have the tools necessary to bring quick relief and clarity to current self-forgiveness issues as they come up. I would certainly recommend this book study to future participants if they are experiencing shame and guilt about themselves and their behavior, past and present."

~Doug R.
Redmond, WA

Brenda Is Flexible and Creative

"Brenda is flexible and creative. Those qualities are especially important to me while I am in need of support by a coach. I personally feel better understood if I email my dilemma ahead of time as a journaling exercise instead of being confused as to what I want from our one-on-one sessions. Sometimes just being heard was all I needed, but if not she offered me the support I needed through her personal radical approach to helping me sort out whatever it was that bothered me. Brenda is a talented coach, and she is committed to her client's growth and well-being. Thanks, Brenda."

~Dean M.
Rockport, TX

I Felt Skeptical

"Before the Forgiveness Ceremony I felt skeptical that such a simple body-mind exercise could work. I appreciated the warm atmosphere Brenda created and her encouraging guidance. I now notice that I am willing to be more open and vulnerable with people and situations I want to forgive and/or seek forgiveness from. I'd recommend this ceremony for anyone who has stuck energy around old wounds and/or wounding others and wants more love and healing in their lives."

~Suzanne S.
Olympia, WA

Remained Calm

"Brenda, I am so grateful for the opportunity of healing on Saturday! I was certainly feeling different energy. Then, first thing Monday morning a situation occurred involving the person I was doing the work on in class Saturday. For the first time, that 'pit in my stomach' did not rise up. I remained calm. My heart didn't start racing. It was a whole different 'energy' when discussing this person than it was in the past. I am now more open and willing to understand my involvement and how to learn/better myself from it. I am a better person since you have come into my life and I am so grateful and appreciative for this blessing!"

~Paula J.
Kirkland, WA

Released from the Pain

"Brenda, I just wanted to say thank you again for our work together. The process you walked me through has absolutely released me from the pain I was carrying. It's a miracle and a blessing."

~Dannielle M
Surrey BC

Giving, Accepting and Supportive

"I have been working with Brenda for the past six months. She has made a huge, positive impact on my feelings and my outlook on life. Brenda has been so giving, accepting and supportive through all the ups and downs I have experienced. She is not afraid to tell you like it is…in the most loving way. She picks up on subtle shifts and wants to celebrate them for the miracles that they are. She is open with her own personal journey, which inspires me to do better and work harder. She is like my own personal cheerleader for life. Brenda wants the best for me and truly cares about how I am doing and feeling. Thanks to Brenda and radical forgiveness, my life is going down a much healthier and happier path. I feel better about myself and my future."

~Lana H.
Mt. Vernon, WA

"I couldn't release the anger and negativity attached to an incident of betrayal that had happened recently in my life. Through the workshop I learned there were so many more layers involved. Brenda helped me sort through the layers and get to the root of being able to forgive.

"Brenda is authentic and passionate in her teachings. She is the real deal when it comes to experience and wisdom. She is very empathetic, which allows you to feel safe and secure in her presence while doing the exercises. You truly feel comfortable working through the processes. I have noticed a huge shift in my own inner peace and calmness as I continue to work through the teachings and exercises. I'm not in inner conflict or turmoil since the workshop. I can sort through my emotions with more calm, which allows me to hear intuitive messages more clearly. I recommend Brenda's workshop if you are harboring any past guilt or bitterness regarding forgiveness or if you are holding on to negative experiences or emotions. She will help you get to the root of your struggles, and to allow yourself to forgive. This is one of the most freeing experiences I have ever had. You will leave the workshop with a whole new frame of mind and emotions."

~Betty S.
Bremerton, WA

Message from the Author

By sharing about myself and my work, I hope to give you comfort in knowing I can guide you through life's challenges.

First, allow me to share this simple perspective: each individual life is indeed a journey. And one of the biggest decisions each of us will ever make is how we wish to spend our life—as a victim, or as a victor.

By continuing along your own, unique journey as a victim, you're always carrying an enormous amount of baggage. That's a lot of heavy lifting for one person to endure. However, if you choose to travel the road of life as a victor, you'll be amazed how much lighter, joyful and fancy-free your journey can be. I know these truths all too well, having lived as both.

For me, life has been a series of recovery processes. Within these experiences, I've learned that recovery, itself is not a destination—it's a process. Yet, many people remain 'stuck' in recovery endlessly.

I specialize in helping women step into their own power—through forgiveness. Having personally experienced abuse, addiction, divorce, major health issues and surgery, I know first-hand the many faces and phases of recovery. Yet, as critically important as recovery is, it's not the ultimate process.

Forgiveness is the key to restoring and maintaining well-being—forgiveness of ourselves, of others and even of life, itself. I guide others through the powerful process of forgiveness using several transformative tools and techniques.

The forgiveness work forever changed me and I feel it is important to understand the depths from which I rose, inspiring the phoenix in my logo.

My 'baggage car' began slowing my train of life down, early on—when I was abandoned at the age of three. This precipitated a life fraught with every imaginable form of abuse, from mental and physical to sexual, even spiritual in nature. This cycle was perpetuated by abusers ranging from friends and lovers to husband(s) and bosses, and last but by no means least, myself.

As a result, that overloaded baggage car slowed my life to a crawl, manifesting itself in eating disorders, addictions, toxic relationships and life-threatening health—among other challenges. I was resigned to a seemingly eternal culture of victimhood. I blamed anyone and everyone but myself. However, that behavior merely ties you to the proverbial tracks—where you run over yourself, over and over again.

But forgiveness has transitioned me from victim to victor. I had already begun my own, personal recovery. Eventually, I studied and became certified in a number of intuitive, healing and recovery modalities—both traditional and untraditional. All of these were integral to becoming the kind of coach I wanted to be—one who truly helps others.

Yet, I didn't truly 'come into my own' until I discovered the power of forgiveness.

Forgiveness gave me the knowledge, confidence and resources to fully embrace the concept of becoming master of my own fate, and moving beyond my scars and challenges—no matter how arduous.

Forgiveness has given me the ability to assist others to step into their own power. I am deeply, genuinely honored and privileged to work with each individual who reaches out to me. By giving me an opportunity to assist you in letting go of your baggage and moving beyond your most ardent challenges, I achieve my life's purpose. Let me help you begin finding and achieving yours.

Brenda

Brenda Reiss

Contents

PART ONE: Forgiving Yourself 21

PART TWO: Forgiving Others 27

PART THREE: Leading a Forgiving Life 57

Forgiving Yourself

Have you ever noticed you can hold onto past slights and mistakes long after they happened? It can be days, weeks, months or even years!

Never fear—forgiveness is a process. As you make your way through the process, there may be progress forward followed by a backslide. That's ok, too, and all part of the program. It varies for everyone but you can get through it.

The first key to self-forgiveness is awareness. You want to be knowledgeable about what you are doing, feeling and thinking in any given moment. When you are aware, you feel alive.

Are you clear on how you show up? Do you find that you get stressed or tense around certain people or situations? How often do you pause to take in what you are feeling and look at the "bigger picture"? By taking a few moments to become aware, you can break patterns that stop you from stepping into your higher self.

Throughout the day you have a running conversation going on in your head as you talk to yourself. It's a good practice to pay attention to what that little voice is saying and question whether what it's saying is true. Also, when it's dismissive or critical, make an attempt to change the words and feeling to love and compassion, as if you were holding a conversation with your best friend.

Most people keep beating themselves up way past the point of usefulness and become unfairly self-critical. Chalk part of it up to our sub-personalities or the meeting table of voices in the head. Ever set your alarm the night before when you were determined to get up and go to the gym and then, when it buzzes, have another voice make a reasonable argument for more pillow time? And then an inner critic jumping in to find fault with that? It's no wonder a person can find herself exhausted by arguing—without having spoken a word!

This is why it's so important to bring perspective—and forgiveness—into the conversation in your head. One thing you can do is appoint an "inner protector" to stick up for you. Train this voice to highlight your good qualities and encourage you to stick to the high road. Forgive yourself and love yourself to help build your self-esteem.

Other things to keep in mind when you find yourself stuck in the past and looking for a way to move on:

Get clear on what you believe. When you know your core values and morals, you identify what's important and then can feel it when things feel in alignment or out of alignment. This means when you err yourself or are wronged by others, you know instantly because it feels out of alignment with how you represent yourself in the world. This will also help reaffirm to yourself that you can handle situations so they feel good to you. The more you do this, the more you'll grow your confidence and self-esteem.

Ask if you are reacting or responding. Much of our life is spent in reaction to others and events around us. We often react without thinking.

It's a gut reaction, many times based in fear and insecurity, which isn't the most appropriate way to act. Responding, on the other hand, is taking the situation in and deciding, calmly, the best course of action we can take based on how we are feeling and mostly on our values. If you want to change your life, you have to take responsibility for your actions and this can be difficult if you are always in a reactive state.

Live in the present. Are you living in the past? There's nothing new there. When you can really recognize that what's done is done, you not only feel better now, you open yourself up to more gifts to come. In addition, you'll live every day in the present more accepting of what is.

Give yourself a break—and a chance for a "do-over." No one is perfect, so lower any standards of perfection you've been using to keep tabs on your own actions. Give yourself some slack if you don't do things right the first time or regret the way you acted in the past. Beating yourself up doesn't help anything. Still feeling bad? To show yourself you've learned something since the mistake, think about or even write down how you would have done things differently if you could go back. It's never too late to get yourself back on the path of forgiveness.

Still need help? Consider coaching to get some perspective and a boost in your self-talk and more. Read books on the subject and surround yourself with supportive people.

Thought & Action Prompts

Identify a place in your body where not forgiving yourself or others is weighing heavily. Where in your body does it reside? What does it feel like? What would it feel like if it wasn't there any longer?

How do you view yourself around the subject of regret or sadness? How would that view change if you took even one step toward forgiveness?

Get in the practice of questioning your self-talk. One technique is when a negative thought comes up ask yourself "is it true?" This powerful question puts a spotlight on the mistaken beliefs you can have about yourself.

Want to sleep better? Before bed, write down at least five things you are grateful for. This simple exercise really does work in putting you in a good frame of mind to rest!

Quotes About Forgiving Yourself

"Forgiveness is me giving up my right to hurt you for hurting me."

– Anonymous

"The weak can never forgive. Forgiveness is the attribute of the strong."

– Mahatma Gandhi

"To forgive is to set a prisoner free and discover that the prisoner was you."

– Louis B. Smedes

"It is never too late to forgive ourselves for our past shortcomings and restore that feeling of excitement to our lives by living them with an attitude of positive expectancy!
Then was then—and now is now."

– Don McArt

"Love yourself just as you want other people to love you... Forgive yourself for past mistakes and allow yourself to experience new opportunities."

– Ryan Cooper

"You cannot change the actions which led you to your situation now, but you can control your actions and thoughts as you move forward. It's important to forgive, and let go."

– C. Felder

"Self-forgiveness is an act of reclaiming your freedom from the past."

– Sandi Amorim

"If you make a mistake, which you undoubtedly will, acknowledge it and forgive yourself. Say comforting things to yourself and tell yourself that a mistake or two do not define you in any way."

– Earl Brandone

"Forgiveness is a true act of trust and love
that you can give yourself."

– James Fullerton

"Although forgiveness can be extremely difficult,
it can be one of the most important things
you do for your overall mental wellbeing."

– Ace McCloud

"I have to forgive myself and learn from it."

— Michael Unks

"Feeling bad about yourself for things that have gone wrong won't change things so forgive yourself and your mistakes and then move on from them."

— Heather Rose

"Offering yourself forgiveness and compassion for what has happened will help you to let go of the past so that you can move more fully into the future."

– Alison Cardy

Forgiving Others

As time marches forward, it's common every once in a while to take stock of where you are in life and what got you there. It's natural to start a running tally of "what I feel good about" and "what I don't."

When forgiveness is missing, offenses that were committed against you, or some pain that you caused others, can replay in your mind over and over and over again. This can cause anger or remorse that is often a recipe for bitterness and bad health. It can also lead to isolation and loneliness. Science has linked this isolation and loneliness to increased health problems and higher mortality.

Time to turn this story around—and it includes forgiving others.

Remember when I talked about forgiving yourself and cutting yourself some slack? It's a good thing to keep in mind in this situation, too. People make decisions in "real time." A number of factors can color their decisions from individual perception of the situation to mood and communication skills (or lack thereof). Adrenalin can kick in leading someone to act out of fear or protection. Or a build-up of stress over time can lead to a bad decision or a few moments acted out in anger that leads to regret. Any of these situations give you an opportunity to give someone else—or yourself—a pass and use it as an opportunity for learning.

Holding on to past hurts and anger can do more than increase health problems—it can also take up a great deal of space in your mind. Trust me, you don't want to rent out this valuable real estate if you don't have to. It's better saved for being your best self and pursuing your own hopes and dreams, along with positive thoughts and better relationships, rather than re-living stops along the low road of life.

Many people mistakenly think if the offending party is forgiven it means their actions or words are condoned. Actually, it has nothing to do with "them," and is rather a gift you give yourself. If forgiveness is a loaded word, some people prefer to think of it as a form of "acceptance," where you are moving forward on your own terms. This idea of acceptance comes from Janice Spring, a clinical psychologist in Westport, Connecticut. It's another way to kick people out from living rent-free in your head and heart.

Keep in mind, when you forgive it's not saying the other person is right. It's saying that you're choosing to forgo anger and resentment for your own health and well-being.

What about approaching others to seek forgiveness or offer it? It means being prepared for rejection or to be rebuffed. But it can also mean an opportunity to heal. Look for opportunities to practice forgiveness and have the courage to address slights, resentments and emotional injuries in ways that are both constructive and healing.

These actions are time sensitive because no one knows how long they have. This is even true for the so-called professionals. There's a story about a therapist who, after getting divorced, became estranged from her former mother-in-law. They didn't speak for two decades. After learning the older woman's husband had died, the therapist decided to call her. The older woman was thrilled.

She admitted she was sad they were no longer friends and also said she didn't understand what happened. After an awkward five minutes when the air was cleared about a misunderstanding that led to the break in friendship, the two picked up where they left off.

The forgiveness continued. Inspired by his daughter, the therapist's 80-year-old father also patched things up with the older woman and they each regained an old friend in their later years. Plus, when the older woman died, she left a favorite piece of art to her former daughter-in-law, a gift that was personally delivered to her by her ex. It did take years for the moment to arrive, however when it did, it benefited all.

It may not always be appropriate to approach the person where forgiveness is asked for or sought, but if the opportunity arises it can lead to a sense of relief and peace that makes life lighter and more satisfying.

I have my own story about forgiving others.

As I was going through my divorce, and before I had discovered the process I now teach, I was working hard on forgiving my soon-to-be ex. I felt hurt, betrayed, fearful, sad, unlovable—you name it. Yet, I knew it was important to forgive so I could move forward. I didn't really know that I needed to forgive myself. My thinking was that the forgiveness needed to be outside of me as that was what I was always told to do and understood it to be.

Now, I thought I was doing pretty darn good but every time I saw a metro bus I would start crying and my heart would ache.

See, my ex was a metro bus driver. So no matter how hard I was trying to forgive him, every time I saw that bus I was being triggered back to the pain and loneliness I felt. Back to feelings of betrayal. And as I felt into those feelings more, it wasn't just with him. It had been with others too. I had felt that same feeling. That's when I made a breakthrough—I identified it as a pattern. When I could recognize that and follow it back in my life, I was able to approach the work on myself through those feelings outside of me.

I allowed my emotions to arrive, be heard and released. So many times I shut my emotions down and didn't allow myself to feel them or even acknowledge them. I didn't learn that it was okay to have emotions. Nothing in my life growing up supported that idea.

Today, I get to support this idea and it feels damn good. Giving voice to what I feel in a safe way and with safe people is healing.

Thought and Action Prompts

One of the blocks to forgiveness is not letting emotions flow freely. Many times this is a result of the way we grow up—we're taught to keep it inside. What is your experience with expressing emotions?

You've probably heard the technique of "writing a letter and not sending it" to express your feelings about being grieved by another. One way this works is getting specific not about the acts committed or not committed, but rather focusing on the feelings involved. In fact, using the writing prompt "I felt…" helps in this exercise.

Sometimes reading the letter to a trusted friend or coach can help identify the root of the issue. For instance, many times the rage isn't directed at another person but ourselves for putting up with a situation.

Quotes About Forgiving Others

"When you hold resentment toward another, you are bound to that person or condition by an emotional link that is stronger than steel. Forgiveness is the only way to dissolve that link and get free."

– Catherine Ponder

"Always forgive your enemies—nothing annoys them so much."

– Oscar Wilde

"We read that we ought to forgive our enemies; but we do not read that we ought to forgive our friends."

– Sir Francis Bacon

"Let us forgive each other—only then will we live in peace."

– Leo Nikolaevich Tolstoy

"We are not perfect, forgive others as you would want to be forgiven."

– Catherine Pulsifer

"Don't get angry quickly—be kind, be forgiving, be patient."

– Patricia Meyers

"Sincere forgiveness isn't colored with expectations that the other person apologize or change. Don't worry whether or not they finally understand you. Love them and release them. Life feeds back truth to people in its own way and time-just like it does for you and me."

– Sara Paddison

"A happy marriage is
the union of two good forgivers."

– Robert Quillen

"Once a woman has forgiven her man,
she must not reheat his sins for breakfast."

– Marlene Dietrich

"We may not know how to forgive, and we may not want to forgive; but the very fact we say we are willing to forgive begins the healing practice."

– Louise Hay

"Like a loving spouse who occasionally doesn't feel so loving, we ask for forgiveness and come back into relationship."

— Laurie Penner

"Chances are someone has hurt you really bad and the only way you will be free from the anger is to forgive them."

— James Robor

"Forgiving others is a practice we should all do more of, it can change your life to one of frustration to one of peace."

– Catherine Pulsifer

"You don't have to accept the invitation
to get angry. Instead, practice forgiveness,
empathy and encouragement."

– Dan Fallon

"Forgiveness is the spirit of forgiving others and let
their mistakes go."

– Ilene Prat

"Forgiving those who wronged you does not justify their actions, or say their behavior was ok. Forgiveness gets you out of prison. When a person is bound by unforgiveness, they are carrying a grudge."

– Nathan D. Pietsch

"Forgiveness opens the opportunity for those relationships to show you the love that you have always deserved."

– Eric Watterson

"Forgiving means letting go of the past. It means that we let others act for themselves without judging them."

– Christian Olsen

Leading A
Forgiving Life

Oftentimes forgiveness is associated with the releasing of anger and resentment. If someone hurt you or caused you harm, at some point you may decide to let go of any ill feelings and put the past behind you. In some cases, this can be enough to move forward and live a happy and healthy life.

But for those that have endured trauma, although they may have forgiven and moved on with life, these feelings, experiences and emotions tend to get buried deep down into the core of their existence, like nothing ever happened. They go on with life, have careers, families, children and on the outside everything appears to be "normal."

On the inside things tends to shows up differently. You may work too much, drink too much, eat too much, don't eat enough; maybe you hurt yourself in private, maybe you talk bad about yourself or maybe you don't believe you deserve happiness. Forgiveness is not just about releasing anger and resentment, it's about cultivating an environment of acceptance and allowance so that you can create the life that you were designed to live.

To live a life of forgiveness it's helpful to identify patterns and categories of things you regret. Many times people tend to focus on specific incidents or traumas, but if you can pull the lens to look at the big picture and find patterns, you're on your way to breaking those patterns. For example, if you have a habit of getting into relationships where the other person is far from loyal, that's a good thing to identify. You can look to yourself to see why you're attracted to people who tend to betray you and look to break that pattern.

(Note, this takes deeper work than I can be cover in these pages. It's best to consult a professional.)

Forgiveness is more than "word deep." It's an active process where you make a decision to let go of negative feelings towards another. It may be hard to see at times, but it is possible to release resentment and anger and instead welcome feelings of empathy, compassion and even affection towards the person and situation. This is a sign of maturity not only of emotions but of thinking and perspective.

It bears repeating, forgiveness is not about denying what was done to you. Instead, it's feeling, sometimes for the first time, the hurt, pain or anger about what happened to you. Even in the middle of all those feelings, you can make a choice to forgive.

People who hang on to grudges are more likely to experience depression and even post-traumatic stress disorder, as well as other dangerous health conditions. Those who forgive more easily, or learn to do so, tend to live a more satisfying life with less depression, stress, anger and anxiety. Which group do you want to be in?

Why would you want to forgive? Because, beyond the physical detriments of not living a life of forgiveness, and the mental room it takes up, it can be something that colors the way you live the rest of your life. You see, even if you're able to push the person or situation away from you, the feelings you're trying to run away from will appear again and again—until you make the decision and take action to feel and release them.

This leads to the realization that forgiveness is a choice. It lies in your power to forgive another or adopt a more forgiving attitude in general. This allows you to benefit from better physical and emotional health—and find it more enjoyable to live with yourself, too. (Remember those voices in your head?)

 You'll come to the point where it's the better choice to accept the past after you've done all you can to amend past mistakes. Turn the page and count those mistakes as part of your story and threads in the tapestry of your life. They make up who you are. Applying a dose of gratefulness, no matter where things stand, goes a long way to healing and allowing you to move on and forgive yourself.

Thought Prompts and Actions

One of my favorite suggestions to greet the day and having a "mindful morning" is to stomp around your bedroom in bare feet and declare "I deserve to be here!"

There's a great thought from Eckhart Tolle that encourages us to say "yes" to life—and see how life starts working for you rather than against you. Look for opportunities throughout your day to say "yes!"

Be OK with the fact that some days will be harder than others, especially if you're going through challenging times. When you do wake up feeling better, acknowledge it and give yourself a pat on the back for doing the deep transformational work that others avoid. It's worth it.

And you are worth it!

Quotes About Forgiveness and Life

"To forgive is the highest,
most beautiful form of love. In return, you will
receive untold peace and happiness."

– Robert Muller

"Forgiveness does not change the past,
but it does enlarge the future."

– Paul Boose

"We are all on a life long journey and the core of its meaning, the terrible demand of its centrality is forgiving and being forgiven."

– Martha Kilpatrick

"Forgiveness is the giving,
and so the receiving, of life."

– George MacDonald

"True forgiveness is not an action after the fact, it is an attitude with which you enter each moment."

– David Ridge

"Forgiveness is a powerful thing.
It doesn't change what has happened;
it changes what is to come."

– Janeen Latini

"We are forgiven as we forgive.
We receive peace within ourselves when we forgive."

– Jason A. Ponzio

"The only way to battle against bitterness in your life is to forgive."

— Kristin N. Spencer

"Forgive so that you may be forgiven.
Keep in mind that letting go of pain from the past
frees you to fully enjoy the blessings of the moment."

– Pearl Little

"There is no love without forgiveness,
and there is no forgiveness without love."

– Bryant H. McGill

"Forgiveness is about cultivating greater understanding, compassion, and love. We accomplish this by releasing that which we are holding to ourselves too closely."

– John Felitto

"Life is so short.
Grudges are a waste of time.
Laugh when you can, apologize when you should,
and trust God with what you cannot change."

– Nicky Gumbel

"Forgiveness takes willingness,
even a determination, a decision if you will."

– Lori Hill

"Once you realize we're all equally capable of doing wonderful or horrible things to those we love, it's easier to plant that seed of forgiveness and allow it to start growing."

– Linda Barbosa

"Remember; forgiveness is not a feeling—
it is a conscious choice."

– Paul Kendall

"To forgive is the highest, most beautiful form of
love. In return, you will receive untold peace and
happiness."

– Robert Muller

To Keep in Mind

As a forgiveness coach, I've identified seven steps along the way to forgiveness:

1. **Openness.** Being open-minded about exploring the process of forgiveness is key to finding a way to make it work in your life. Those who remain closed to the idea have a much more difficult time of moving on.

2. **Awareness.** Having an awareness of yourself and what role you play in your life situations is important to finding forgiveness. It's not a case of blaming or shaming, but rather looking at things from the perspective of awareness.

3. **Willingness.** Ah, the ability to entertain the idea of change. Willingness is so important in life in general, and especially so related to forgiveness. I think of it as putting yourself in the starting blocks of forgiveness. Are you willing to do so?

4. **Responsibility.** The "R" word here is not about accepting responsibility for wrong-doing (although you can if you want) but rather taking responsibility for yourself and the way you feel. Blaming and shaming will get you no-where.

5. **Trust.** Learning how to trust again is a big step forward in the forgiveness process. It may not come overnight, but you can get to a place of trusting others and yourself again.

6. **Releasing patterns.** Many times the monkey mind of shame, guilt and limiting beliefs takes hold and keeps you in its grip for years. Look for opportunities to think differently and question what's not serving you in these areas.

7. **Taking action.** You can get yourself on the proper path through forgiveness. It can mean choosing differently and consciously creating your life. Taking action can be one of the boldest things you ever do—and so worth it!

Get More of Brenda!

Download the free eBook
"11 Steps to Forgiveness"

Discover the key steps to bring about more joy in life.

In this book you will find how to:

- Bring more joy and peace to life.

- Practice healing through forgiveness.

- Use proven tools and techniques for getting started today!

Get the free eBook at **www.BrendaReissCoaching.com**

CPSIA information can be obtained
at www.ICGtesting.com
Printed in the USA
FSOW04n0307091117
40940FS